Stock Market Investing f...

Learn These Simple Strategies in Le... ...o ivimutes, and Make Money for the Rest of Your Life - Your Personal Roadmap to Financial Freedom

Table of Contents

INTRODUCTION 5

CHAPTER 1: THE FUNDAMENTALS OF THE STOCK MARKET 9

   How Does the Stock Market Work? 12
      Stocks 15
      Common stock 16
      Preferred stock 16
      Penny Stocks 16
      Blue Chip Stocks 17
      Primary Market 17
      Secondary Markets 17
      Over-The-Counter Markets 18
      Bid 18
      Ask 18
      Spread 18
      Volatility 19
      Dividend 19
      Broker 19
      Bear Market 19
      Bull Market 20
      Beta 20
      Index 20
   The Law of Supply and Demand 20
   Why Invest in the Stock Market 22

CHAPTER 2: GETTING STARTED 27

   Passive vs Active Investing 28
      Active Investing 28
      Passive Investing 30
   Stocks vs Mutual Funds 31
      Mutual Funds & EFTs 31
      How do mutual funds make you money 33
      Individual Stocks 34
   The Importance of Diversification 35
   Managing Your Portfolio 37
   Tips for Success 41

CHAPTER 3: TOOLS AND PLATFORMS 46

Choosing the Right Trading Platform 46
TD Ameritrade 49
E*TRADE 50
Fidelity 50
Stock Research Tools 51
Stock screeners 52
Price and Volume 53
Moving Average Lines 54
Relative Strength Line 55
1. Understanding the trend 55
2. Understanding the story behind the chart 56
3. Look for support or resistance 57
Top 3 Most Profitable Chart Patterns 58
I. Cup with handle 59
II. Double Bottom 59
Stock Simulators 61
What to Look for in a Stock Research Tool 62
The Best Stock Research Tools 64

CHAPTER 4: STRATEGIES FOR LONG TERM SUCCESS 68

When to Buy 69
1. Market direction 69
2. Look at the market fundamentals 71
3. Look at the chart action 72
When to Sell 73
1. Go for gains that range from 20 -25% 73
2. Limit your losses using the 8% sell rule 74
3. Take profits when a stock crashes through a rising trend line 75
Staying Ahead of the Curve 75
1. Dollar-cost averaging 76
2. Growth Investing 78
3. Prioritize managed funds over individual stocks 79
The 4-Step Routine for Picking Winners 81
1. Gather your research tools 82
2. Narrow your focus 82
3. Get into the qualitative research 83

4. Build a well-informed narrative *85*
CONCLUSION **88**

Introduction

If you are not planning on working yourself to the grave, chances are you think about investing for your future constantly. You ask yourself *Am I ready? When should I start? How do I start? Where do I start?* If this sounds like you, relax, you are not alone. Many have found themselves at this same crossroad asking themselves the same questions, including, of course, yours truly.

When I first had the idea to invest in the stock market, the doubts came in fast and furious. How could I, an average Joe, muster the intricacies of the stock market? Before that point, like many others, I had considered the stock market to be the preserve of well-heeled business moguls and business savvy wall street types. Fortunately, it did not take long for me to find out that my doubts were not only unfounded but also completely untrue.

The stock market is not only one of the most accessible investment avenues, but it is also surprisingly affordable.

If you have been putting off investing until you reach a certain magical number, it is time to ditch the myth that you need to be rich to invest in stocks. Every day millions of retail investors join the stock market as investors with as little as $500. So if your excuse so far has been a lack of capital, you may need to find a new one. Stock market trading is accessible to anyone provided you are willing to educate yourself and commit to investing consistently.

Granted, there is a lot of knowledge that traders need to equip themselves with but this is the kind of knowledge that you can easily learn. The sole purpose of this book is to provide you with all the information that you need to get started in stock market trading. From all the trading jargon that you are bound to come across to the ABCs of the stock market, you will find detailed information herein that will equip you with the basics of how the stock market works and why you should invest in it.

We will also take you through how to get started as a stock market investor. There are tips for both active and passive investors so whichever approach works for you, there is plenty of useful information for you in this book. Ultimately the bulk of this book is on trading tools and strategies that will help you build wealth over time by trading stocks. We understand that as an investor, the stock market will only be useful to you if you can make returns on your investment. That is why we have outlined beginner-friendly strategies that will see you build an impressive investment portfolio.

This book is for the average person who wants to invest in the stock market and do so wisely. It is meant to equip you with effective tools and strategies to use as an investor in the stock market. No matter what your financial goals are, the stock market presents plenty of opportunities for long term gains for the discerning trader. If you are ready to start building your nest egg and secure your financial future, keep reading, and find out just how easy it is to do just that.

Chapter 1: The Fundamentals of The Stock Market

Delayed gratification is a strong suit that few have and this is why investing has always been a challenge for many. You want to make money but not in a decade or a couple of years, but right now. Ponzi schemes aside, profitable investments that can actually build you wealth for a lifetime take time and lots of patience. These two things are probably the most important tools that any beginner in stock market investing needs to be aware of.

Our motivations for investing may differ but ultimately all investments have one goal in common; to make a return or profit on the investment. You may be eyeing early retirement, you may be in it for the financial freedom or maybe you are just sick of having your money sitting in a savings account attracting point nothing interest. Regardless of what your goals are, the idea behind investing is that you use your money to make more money.

The stock market presents a unique opportunity for both retail and corporate investors because anyone can do it at any scale. You can invest as little as $1000 or as much as a million dollars. There is room and opportunity for everyone to get in and make a decent return on their investment. That said, the stock market is not the way to go if you want quick money. Stocks like most other investments have one thing in common; they depend on the power of time.

Time is your biggest ally when it comes to investing. If you have been waiting for a magical moment when you will have "enough" money to start investing, the bad news is that you will probably never have "enough" money and the other bad news is that the right time to start investing was yesterday.

A common misconception that most people have is that you need to have a lot of money to start investing. In actual fact people who invest do not necessarily have more money than you, they simply make investing a priority. And because they make investing a priority, they end up having more money than you. See how that works?

Unlike consumption, investment takes money out of your pocket and puts it towards your future. When you can think of investment as an insurance policy to safeguard your financial future then the decision on when and if to invest becomes pretty much a no-brainer. Nobody wants to be cash strapped forever or have to work themselves to the grave because they did not put their money to work when they had the chance.

The beauty of this golden age of technology that we live in is that anyone with the will and determination to do so can access all the tools they need to start investing in the stock market. This ease of accessibility coupled with its affordability has made the stock market increasingly popular with retail investors. With just a few a hundred dollars you can find an online brokerage at the click of a button and get started as an investor in the stock market. Yes, it is that easy. Before you jump on the bandwagon however, it is important to understand what you are investing in. The natural starting point is of course understanding how the stock market works.

How Does the Stock Market Work?

It is no coincidence that most people who have wealth have a big part of this wealth invested in stocks. Stocks carry their fair share of risks for any investor but when done right, stock market investing can be one of the most efficient ways to build and retain wealth.

A stock market is an exchange where people trade by buying and selling shares on traded companies. Once you have bought shares in a company your stock gives you ownership of a small part of that company. With this ownership, the value of your investment will be determined by the movements of the price of the company's shares. If for instance you bought Apple stocks and the price moves up while you are holding the stock then the value of your investment increases. On the other hand, if the price of the Apple stocks decreases while you are holding the stocks, the value of your investment decreases.

The price of a stock is driven by the forces of supply and demand. Naturally, when the demand for a particular stock is higher than the supply the price of that stock will increase. In much the same way when the supply is higher than the demand then the price of that stock will decrease. In essence, the stock price is a reflection of the value as set by the market conditions. When you buy a stock as an investor your general goal is to make money when the price of the stock increases. This is why a big part of investing in the stock market is knowing how to select the right stocks to buy.

When the price of the shares you have appreciates, you can sell your shares at a profit. This means that you will get a return on your investment and you can reinvest your capital back into the market or you can cash out. The beauty of stock market investing is that there is usually no limit to how long you can hold your investment. You can keep your shares for 20 years or you can choose to sell them when the share price appreciates. This will ultimately depend on what your end goal is.

Price appreciation is not the only way to make money in the stock market. Dividends are payments made out to shareholders when a company makes a profit. This means depending on the type of shares that you have you will receive dividends from the company whose shares you hold.

For instance, if you bought Tesla stocks and the company pays out dividends quarterly to their shareholders, you will get a percentage of these dividends based on the value of your shares. You can choose to take these dividends as a cash payment or you can choose to reinvest them back into the company by buying more shares.

It is important to note that not all companies pay dividends. This means that if you want to make money in the stock market by earning regular dividends you will need to understand the type of stocks to buy and which company's stocks will get you dividends.

Stock exchanges like the NYSE (New York Stock Exchange), Nasdaq, the Tokyo Stock Exchange are some of the largest exchanges. However, stocks are also sold in over-the-counter markets where they trade directly through brokers and not in open exchanges like the NYSE. These markets are referred to as secondary markets where investors trade stocks by buying and selling amongst themselves.

Basic Terms and Concepts

Stocks

A stock is a share of ownership in a company. Stocks are also referred to as shares. When you buy a stock you acquire a fraction of ownership of the company whose shares you have bought. When you buy stocks, you become a shareholder in the particular company and the percentage or size of your shares will determine the dividends you can earn.

Investors in the stock market can make money from their stocks in different ways. You can earn money in the form of dividends paid out on the shares you own. You can also earn money by selling your shares or stocks.

Common stock

Common stocks give you ownership of a company based on the number of shares you own. Common stocks are the most basic type of shares to own and they entitle you to dividends where applicable and voting rates proportionate to the shares you own.

Preferred stock

Preferred stocks entitle you to a fixed dividend rate for your shares. With this type of stock, you earn dividends before shareholders who have common stock but you do not get voting rights. Unlike shareholders of common stocks, preferred stocks give you a guarantee that you will receive dividends on your stock.

Penny Stocks

A penny stock is a stock that trades for less than $5 per share. Penny stocks are typically short-term holdings where you want to take advantage of price movements in volatile markets. Penny stocks investing work for short term investors who do not plan to hold the stocks for long periods.

Blue Chip Stocks

Blue-chip stocks are shares of large established corporations that have solid reputations in the market. Blue-chip stocks are characterized by solid balance sheets and steady cash flows. Most blue-chip stocks have a history of earning increasing dividends for their shareholders. These types of stocks are ideal for long term investors who want to hold stocks for long periods.

Primary Market

In a primary market, companies sell their shares directly to the investors. In most cases, companies in primary markets sell to corporations and institutions rather than to individual investors. Hedge funds, mutual funds, and similar investors are typically the kind of investors that buy shares directly from companies in primary markets.

Secondary Markets

In a secondary market, investors buy and sell shares amongst themselves. Individuals investors buy shares in secondary markets. In this type of market, you can choose to buy shares of a particular company or a mix of different companies shares in exchange-traded funds or EFTs.

Over-The-Counter Markets

OTC markets are where companies that are not listed in exchanges like NYSE trade their shares. In OTC markets there is no public price for the shares and the value of the transaction is dependent on the buyer and seller.

Bid

A bid is the price at which you want to buy the share.

Ask

The ask is the price at which the seller wants to sell the share at

Spread

The spread is the difference between the bid and sell prices of a stock. If you want to buy a stock at $50 and the buyer wants to sell it at $45, the spread, in this case, is $5.

Volatility

Volatility refers to the movement of share prices in the market. When the price fluctuates widely within short periods of time then it is said to be highly volatile. The higher the volatility of a particular share, the higher the risk associated with it and also the higher the profit potential.

Dividend

A dividend is the percentage of a company's earnings that is paid out to shareholders. Dividends can be paid out annually or quarterly depending on the company. Not all companies pay dividends to the shareholders.

Broker

A broker is a trader who buys and sells shares for an investor for a fee or commission.

Bear Market

A bear market refers to a downward trend in the market where stock prices are falling

Bull Market

A bull market refers to an upward trend in the market where stock prices are rising.

Beta

Beta is the measurement of the price of a stock relative to the movement of the whole market. If a stock moves 1.5 points for every 1-point move in the market, then it has a beta of 1.5.

Index

An index is a measure that is used as a benchmark to gauge market performance. Some of the most famous indices include the Dow Jones and the S&P 500.

The Law of Supply and Demand

For any transaction to occur there must be a buyer and supplier. This concept also applies to the stock market. In the stock market, there are investors who want to buy shares and there are those who want to sell those shares. In any given market the laws of supply and demand will have a bearing on the price of the particular commodity being traded. Shares that are in high demand like blue-chip stocks will always cost more than penny stocks which have far less demand.

The price of shares in the stock market is determined by the number of buyers and sellers in the market. When the buyers outnumber the sellers, naturally the price trends upwards. In a downward trending market, they will usually be more sellers than there are buyers. This law of demand and supply is one of the factors that determine share prices in the market.

However, other factors including the economic status, political climate, interest rates, and even the management profile of a company will all have an impact on the price of a particular share. These factors are why analysis and research are important when picking the right shares to invest in. Ideally, you want to invest shares that are likely to appreciate in value because this will result in an increase in the value of your investment. Picking the wrong shares can tank your investment especially if your portfolio is not diversified.

Ultimately there is no fool-proof or risk-proof investment but being aware of market trends and factors that are likely to affect share prices is key when investing in the stock market. Stock prices change for a variety of reasons and while you may not always be able to predict market trends, using market indicators such as past price movements and charts can help you determine the right time to buy or sell.

Why Invest in the Stock Market

1. High returns on investments

Let's face it, the only reason you are investing is that you want to make money. Investing in the stock market has helped more people create long term wealth than most other forms of investment. The stock market has averaged a 10% interest on investment per annum since the 1920s which means that even with the associated risks, it is still one of the most effective ways of building wealth over time.

Stocks unlike keeping your money in cash means that the value of your money goes up. In comparison money sitting in cash erodes in value. Stocks have historically proven to be a more reliable and effective way of building wealth over time because of the appreciation that happens with time.

2. The magic of compound interest

When you invest in stocks the compound interest on your investment can translate to huge returns over time. Consider what would happen if a modest annual investment of about $10,000 earns a 7% interest per annum. Over 30 years this amount will be well over a million dollars. Stocks are a great way to benefit from the effect of compound interest on your investment over time.

3. Easy access and affordability

To start trading in stocks all you need to do is sign up with an online trading broker. This is a simple straight forward process that will not require lots of time or effort on your time. Investing in stocks is relatively easy and affordable. You can start with as little capital as $1000 and build your portfolio over time.

This means that anyone willing to get started as a stock market investor simply needs to do a bit of research and find a broker to work with. Ultimately this is much easier than investing in ventures such as real estate or businesses that require huge amounts of capital, time, and energy.

4. Stocks are a great way to save for retirement

Building a nest egg takes time and patience and investing in stocks is one of the best ways to do it. Securing your financial future is probably one of the most important things you can do early on and with stocks, this dream is well within your reach. Investing stocks allows you to grow your wealth steadily and gradually over time.

5. Earn a steady income with dividends

Blue-chip stocks are a great investment for people who not only want to benefit from the increasing value of the investment but also earn a regular income. Dividends are paid out to shareholders periodically and this means that while your money is working for you, you are still getting something out of it. When you earn dividends on your shares it means you do not have to wait years to start enjoying the returns on your investment.

6. Stocks are easy to liquidate

When you invest in stocks, you can easily turn your shares into cash when needed. In case of a rainy day, stocks are easy to liquidate and you can turn your shares into cash in no time. This kind of flexibility makes investing in shares a great option because, well, you never know when you may need to turn your investments into cash.

7. Investing in stocks allows you to outrun inflation

It is no secret that money loses value over time due to factors such as inflation. Investing in stocks can help you save for a major asset such as your first home without having to deal with the impact of inflation on your savings.

Chapter 2: Getting Started

The first rule of investing is to never invest money that you need to live on. This means that whatever you set aside for stock market investing should be money you can afford to put aside for a while and in the worst-case scenario, lose. This may seem like a trivial detail but it will have a major impact on the kind of mindset you take with you to trade. If all your life savings are on the line, that will interfere with your mindset and in most cases will lead you to make questionable trading decisions.

Figuring out how much you want to invest and what your main goal is should be the first step before you get started. A general rule of thumb is to not invest money that you will need in less than five years. This is because stock market investing relies on time to build the value of your investments. Are you saving for retirement? Are you looking to raise money for something 5 0r 10 years down the line? Whatever your goal is, it is always crucial that you go into stock market investing with a clear objective.

Passive vs Active Investing

When it comes to investing in the stock market there are different options available to you. You can choose to be an active investor where you work with an online brokerage and select the shares and stocks you want to invest in yourself. This option works if you have a working knowledge of the stock market and you are looking to do your own research and analysis then choose and buy your own stocks.

Active Investing

If you choose to be an active investor, you will need to find a brokerage. An online brokerage account will provide you with the access you need to purchase stocks and funds. While there are plenty of online brokers to pick from, you need to find one who will suit your needs.

For a beginner in the stock market, these are the most important factors to keep in mind when selecting a broker.

- Account fees
- Commissions

- Investment selection – the more the range of commission-free EFTs that the broker offers the better
- Investor research tools available

As an active investor, you can choose to open an Individual Retirement Account (IRA), or alternatively, you can choose to go with a taxable brokerage account. As the name suggests, a taxable brokerage account will not offer you any tax breaks. However taxable brokerage accounts allow you to trade as much as you want and take your money out whenever you want.

An IRA on the other hand is the appropriate type of investment account if you are investing for retirement. It comes with tax advantages that will benefit your retirement savings. However, on the flip side, an IRA account has restrictions on how much you can invest annually as well as on when and how much you can withdraw from your account.

Setting up a brokerage account online is quick and easy. Once you have decided on the type of investment account you want, you will need to open the account with your broker of choice and initiate a deposit. Once your brokerage account is funded you can start investing your money.

Passive Investing

If you want to invest in the stock market but would rather have someone manage your investment portfolio, you have the option of using Robo-advisers. A Robo-advisor is a service that provides investment management at a fee. A Robo advisor will create an investment portfolio for you based on your objectives, and risk tolerance. When you choose to be a passive investor you will not get to choose stocks and funds yourself as the Robo advisor will do it for you.

Passive investment is a great option for beginners just starting out on the stock market. Since Robo advisors use algorithms to come with the ideal portfolio mix, your risk exposure is managed and you do not have to do your own analysis or research since the stocks and funds to invest in are picked for you. Most Robo-advisors will typically charge 0.25% of your account balance.

Robo advisors also offer just like online brokerages also offer retirement accounts and taxable brokerage accounts. Just as you would in active investing, you should go for an IRA if your primary goal for investing is saving for retirement. The taxable brokerage account is more flexible than the IRA in terms of how much you can invest and withdrawing your money from the account.

Stocks vs Mutual Funds

Mutual Funds & EFTs

If you have chosen to be an active investor, you will need to understand the difference between stocks and stock mutual funds or EFTs. Exchange-traded funds allow you to buy different stocks in a single transaction. When you buy mutual funds or EFTs you are investing in a company that has shares in other companies. This means that when you buy EFTs you will not own the stocks that the fund purchases directly but you will share in the fund's losses and profits.

Mutual funds and EFTs work based on the concept of pooled fund investing. This kind of pooled funds come with the benefit of a diversified portfolio. This means that when you choose to invest in mutual funds you will be investing in a variety of stocks from different companies as opposed to individual stocks. Most investors who choose mutual funds do so because they offer diversification and economies of scale which translate into lower transaction costs for you as the investor.

While both mutual funds and EFTs offer investors pooled fund investors, mutual funds tend to be more complex. Most investors go for EFTs because they are actively traded throughout the trading day meaning that you can trade and monitor your portfolio in real-time. EFTs are usually a great option for beginners in the stock market. Not only do they offer you a diverse portfolio which means lower risk exposure, but they also come with lower management fees since they typically do not require stock analysis.

If your primary goal for investing is retirement, investing in mutual funds and EFTs is always the better choice as opposed to investing in individual stocks.

How do mutual funds make you money

Beginners are encouraged to start their foray into the stock market by investing in pooled funds. So how exactly will these kinds of funds make you money?

1. Through dividends – when you invest in mutual funds you will get dividends on your investment. These dividends can be paid out to you or reinvested back in the fund depending on your preference.

2. Capital gains – When the fund you have invested in sells a security at a profit, this is referred to as a capital gain. These gains are passed on to you as the investor. Most funds distribute capital gains annually to their investors.

3. Net Asset Value – As the price of the stocks that the fund has invested in appreciates with time, so does the

value of your investment. This means that when you decide to sell you will make a return on your investment since it will be higher in value than when you first started investing in the fund.

Individual Stocks

When you want to purchase stocks of a particular company such as GE or Apple, this is basically what investing in individual stock means. You purchase stocks of a particular company and you become a shareholder of that company. This means you can earn dividends on the shares you have purchased. When you purchase individual stocks, you can also hold on to them until the price of the shares appreciates then sell them at a profit.

The risk potential when you invest in individual stocks is higher than the risk associated with EFTs. However, on the plus side, the profit potential is also higher with individual stakes. With greater risk comes greater reward so individual stocks are preferable for investors who are more risk-tolerant. If you choose to invest in individual stocks, you will need to understand market trends and research the companies whose stock you want to buy. Fortunately, most online brokers provide tools that help investors in conducting research and analysis.

The Importance of Diversification

In any investment risk management is a crucial part of the process. When it comes to stock market investing diversification is one of the most effective ways to manage your risk and ensure that your money nets you returns on your investment and not losses. Markets are unpredictable and you cannot avoid market downturns entirely no matter how thorough your analysis and research are. Wise investors do not bank on the markets going their way all the time; they build diversified portfolios that will not be wiped out by a single stock crashing.

So how do you diversify your portfolio as a beginner? Well, for starters, start by investing in mutual funds or EFTs. Pooled securities are already diversified since the fund you invest in will have shares in different companies. This means that your investment is not tied to the success of one particular stock and that you stand to benefit from different securities doing well in the market.

The beauty of diversification is that you can combine both EFTs and individual stock investments in your portfolio. This means that you can invest 80 to 90% of your portfolio in EFTs and the remaining 10% in individual stocks. By doing this you are actively managing your risk exposure while still being able to invest both in funds and individual stocks.

When it comes to investing in individual stocks, the safest way to do it is gradually. Once you have invested most of your portfolio in EFTs or mutual funds, make sure that individual stocks are only a small percentage of your portfolio. When you are starting out it is best to take a small position on a single stock. Gradually add more individual stocks to your portfolio as you get more experience in the stock market. Do not overinvest in a single stock no matter how optimistic you feel about it.

Managing Your Portfolio

Once you have started investing, you will need to manage your portfolio. When you invest in the stock market your view should be long term. This means that while you should keep an eye on your investments and market trends, fretting over inevitable daily fluctuations is counterintuitive.

1. Manage your costs

When you invest you want to make money not lose money. Fees, commissions, and other costs can add up to a tidy sum so every investor needs to be aware of transaction fees, commissions, and any other fees you are paying to invest. This means from the get-go when you are choosing the right broker, commissions and fees should be one of the considerations you keep in mind.

Most beginners find themselves tempted to buy and sell regularly in response to market trends. Resist the urge to do this. The more you transact the more costs and fees you pay and ultimately your investment should take a long-term view. Contrary to popular belief, frequent trading will not make you more money because as we have already stated, time is the biggest ally you have when it comes to stock market investing.

2. Discipline

Profitable investment takes discipline and consistency in terms of sticking to your plan and budget. Put money into your portfolio regularly to make sure it keeps growing. Maintaining discipline and putting money into your investment regularly is one of the most effective ways to build a nest egg. If you keep your consistency you will see your portfolio gradually increase and this growth will also translate into higher returns on your investment.

One of the easiest ways to get wiped out is by treating stocks like lottery tickets. When you jump on the bandwagon whenever there is a new market trend you are very likely to lose your investment. A disciplined investor avoids making rash decisions based on inevitable fluctuations. Your aim should be to invest in stocks that will appreciate over time, hold on to them long term, and let time do the rest. Speculating is not a strategy that will net you good results in the stock market. Keep your discipline by thinking long term.

While job losses and other economic factors may derail your plan, it is always important to get back onto your investment plan as soon as possible. Remember that stock market investing is a long-term plan, this means you are bound to encounter hurdles along the way but they should not deter you from your investment plan.

3. Rebalance once a year

As a new investor, it may be hard to avoid monitoring your portfolio fulltime. However, it is recommended that you avoid readjusting your portfolio too often. Rebalancing once a year will give you a more accurate indication of how your investments are doing. Market fluctuations will alter the percentages of your portfolio allocated to different categories so you can always rebalance this percentage to match the initial plan for your portfolio.

There are several ways to rebalance your portfolio. You can purchase new shares of funds that have dropped below the target percentage you had set using new money you have saved throughout the year. Alternatively, you can also rebalance your portfolio by selling shares that have performed well and then reinvesting in those that underperformed.

4. Diversify

The importance of diversifying your portfolio cannot be over-emphasized. The more you diversify your portfolio the lower your risk exposure. Investing in stocks across a broad spectrum is crucial if you want to grow your investment. This is easily achieved by ensuring that the bulk of your portfolio is invested in mutual funds or EFTs.

Your investment in individual stocks should make up a minimal percentage of your investment portfolio. A good rule to live by when it comes to individual stocks is to ensure that you do not invest more than 5% of your portfolio on one stock. Aim to invest in conservative stocks with regular dividends and term growth potential.

Avoid having a portfolio that is overly skewed towards one sector. Diversification should not just be limited to the type of stocks you buy but should also include geographical diversification. The stock market gives you access to global markets so it is important to include some international stocks in your portfolio.

Tips for Success

1. Use dollar-cost averaging

Dollar-cost averaging means taking a gradual approach to your investments. This means that if you have $5000 to invest, you start by investing $100 into an index fund then making monthly contributions to the fund. This approach allows you to buy into a market at different times which eliminates the risk of buying into a position at the top of the market.

For instance, if a particular index is trading at $100 this month, it could depreciate to $90 by the next month. This means that if you buy into this position all at once at its high point of $100 you will end up spending more than if you bought into it gradually. Cost averaging ensures is easy to set up and ensures that you do not need to be overly concerned about when to but because you are buying in at different times over an extended period.

2. Start with mutual funds and Efts

EFTs and mutual funds are the ideal choice of investment for beginners in stock market investing. These types of pooled funds offer built-in diversification that helps in managing risks and ensuring that your investment is safe. Since pooled funds are professionally managed, you do not have to worry about selecting stocks or picking the right time to buy or sell. EFTs are a relatively easy and hassle-free way for novices to invest in the stock market.

Index funds and EFTs also tend to have low minimums which means that you can start investing with as little as $500. Some brokers even offer index funds with no minimums at all which ensures that no matter how little the capital you have is, you have an opportunity to get started in the stock market.

3. Focus on the long term

Stock investing is a long-term investment strategy. When you get into stocks, your aim should be to build wealth over time. This means that you should be prepared to invest for extended periods in order to reap the benefits of time on your investment. Do not expect to become rich overnight in stocks as the stock markets rarely work this way. By sticking with stocks that have long term potential and periodic gains in terms of dividends, you will stand a better chance than someone who is speculating and trying to make a quick buck by trading stocks.

4. Educate Yourself

If you have chosen to go with mutual funds and EFTs then you do not really need to fret about analysis and picking the right stock or the right time to buy or sell. However, if you plan to trade actively in individual stocks educating yourself on market trends, the different types of analysis, and picking the right stocks to invest in is crucial.

Most brokers will offer trading tools that investors can use to learn more about investing. Take advantage of the wealth of resources available online to keep yourself up to date with knowledge on the intricacies of the stock market. Like most other situations, experience over time will help you to build your knowledge in the stock market. However, for a beginner, it is important to take the time to educate yourself on the ins and outs of the stock market before you start investing in it.

Chapter 3: Tools and Platforms

Technology may have its drawbacks but any investor will tell you that taking advantage of stock trading technology is essential. From smartphone apps to entire websites and even apple watch alerts there is a myriad of resources available to help you with analysis and research of stocks. If you are going to trade actively in the stock market, having the right tools at your disposal can make a significant difference to your bottom line.

As a novice, you will need to make sure that you are getting started on the right foot and this means choosing your trading platform and tools wisely. Making the right moves in the stock market will come down to picking the best stocks to buy and knowing the right time to buy or sell; and this is essentially what the right stock research tools will help you do.

Choosing the Right Trading Platform

Stock market trading is complex enough without having to deal with complicated trading platforms. There are many different trading platforms available and different brokers will have different types of platforms available for their users. Since you will be making your trades through the trading platform, it is essential that you pick a platform that is easy to use but also comes with the tools that you need to inform your trades.

As an investor, you want a trading platform that makes your job easier not harder. So, what exactly are the hallmarks of a good trading platform?

1. User-friendly interphase; Look for a platform that is easy to navigate and one that you can use with ease. Tools and other features should be easy to access and you should be able to execute trades in real-time.

2. Access to research and market analysis tools; market analysis tools will be the most important sources of the information that will guide you on which stocks to buy, the right time to buy and sell and keep you updated with the latest market trends. A good trading platform will have a wide variety of trading tools for technical analysis and fundamental analysis.

3. Access to educational materials; good trading platforms come with a host of other educational benefits for their investors. As a new investor, the availability of educational resources should be top of your list when picking the right trading platform. You want to build your knowledge of the stock market and educational resources are the way to do that. Go for trading platforms that offer courses for their investors, progress tracking, quizzes, and other types of educational benefits.

4. Receive market signals; good trading platforms will send you timely market signals that will guide you on when making your trades. Some platforms will send you signals via email or their mobile apps. These signals will give you indications on time frames, desired markets, and trends. Since these signals come from expert traders, they are extremely helpful tools, especially for beginners.

5. Low-fees; transaction costs can add up over time. go for a trading platform with competitive fees that will not eat into your investment capital. Remember the main advantage of an online platform is that it allows you to trade directly without needing to go through a broker. It should, therefore, be a cost-effective option for people who do not want to pay fees and commissions to brokers.

If you want to know some of the best trading platforms here is a list of the top five beginner-friendly online trading platforms.

TD Ameritrade

TD Ameritrade is widely regarded as one of the best overall trading platforms for beginners. Here are some of the reasons why this platform stands out.

Key features

- Easy to navigate user-friendly interphase
- A simulated trading feature that allows investors to practice trading
- No minimum deposit requirements

- Plenty of educational materials and tools
- Stock trades are free

*E*TRADE*

This is another platform that is ideal for novice traders. It offers a fast interphase that is seamless and pretty easy to navigate. It offers simulated trading for beginners to practice trading without using their funds. This platform also has a host of educational materials to help you get your stock market knowledge up to speed. E-trade has no minimum deposit requirement.

Fidelity

This platform is great for investors who want a platform that offers plenty of on-site learning resources. Fidelity offers a host of research and educational tools that any beginner will find useful. They do not require a minimum deposit and stock trades are usually free on this platform.

Charles Schwab

This platform is popular for its research tools and the educational resources available for beginners. This online platform specializes in retirement and is a great pick if your main goal in investing is to build a nest egg for retirement. This platform does not require a minimum deposit to open an account and as an added plus, all stock trades are free.

Stock Research Tools

If you are going to invest in the stock market, stock research is par for the course. Research is what guides you on what stocks to buy, which to sell, and when to make your trades. Essentially your trading strategy and game plan will be determined to a large extent by the research tools that you use.

Consider what you do when shopping for a car. Sure, the technical specs are important but you also want to know how the car feels on the road, whether the color suits your needs, and even what kind of value adds come with the car. Purchasing the stock is much the same way in that you cannot you're your decision on only one aspect. There are several factors to consider and this is why it is so important to have the best research tools at your disposal.

Here are the main types of stock research tools;

Stock screeners

The sheer volume of stocks available in the stock market means that picking the rights stocks to focus on is not a walk in the park. This is why traders use tools like stock screeners. Stock screeners are tools that scan the entire market and provide you with information such as trading volume, chart patterns, prices, and any other criteria you set.

For instance, if you want to see all the stocks available that are trading under $10 and have a trading volume of half a million shares, you can use a stock screener to filter this information for you. In essence, a stock screener acts as a filter that helps you to narrow down your search by showing you stocks that meet your preferred criteria.

There are plenty of stock screeners available free of charge online including Stock Fetcher, Google Finance, Stock Rover, and many more. You will also find that most online trading platforms have screeners for EFTs and mutual funds. Screeners are useful as a tool but this does not mean you should use them as the only basis for analysis. Think of stock screeners as a starting point to give you a list of stocks to choose from then work your way from there.

Stock Charts

If you are going to invest in individual stocks, stock charts are one of the most important research tools that you should muster. Charts plot the prices traded for a particular stock over a specified period of time. This information helps you identify trends which are the indicators that show you when to buy, when to sell and whether you should invest in that particular stock at all.

When looking at a stock chart, the three main pieces of information you need to watch are:

I.   Price and volume
II. Moving average lines
III. The relative strength line (RS)

Price and Volume

Price is important when trying to understand how a stock is moving. However, you will only get the full story when you look at the share price in relation to the trading volume of the particular share.

When you only focus on the price you will not have a clear picture of how heavy the buying or selling is. The volume of trade shows you what the big investors are doing and tells you whether to sit tight or make a move. For instance, if the price of a stock falls by 5% but the trading volume is below average, it is a clear indication that the large investors are not selling aggressively. This is an indicator that you should sit tight and wait.

Moving Average Lines

When reading charts, you will need to observe the price movement of a stock over a period of time. This movement is tracked by the moving average line. How a stock performs around the moving average line will show you whether it is gaining support or finding resistance.

When the large investors are supporting a stock, they will keep it from falling below the moving average line by adding to their positions. On the flip side, a stock that is finding resistance will fall below the moving average line. When a stock falls below the moving averages line in heavy trading, this is an indication that the big investors are not buying it and neither should you.

Relative Strength Line

The RS line compares the performance of a stock against the performance of the S&P 500. If the RS line is rising then that should tell you that the particular stock is outperforming the market and is, therefore, a good stock to invest in. If the RS line is trending downward then the stock in question is underperforming and it may not be the best time to invest in it.

If you are a novice to the stock market, chart reading may seem intimidating but the key to reading charts is to answer these three questions.

1. What is the trend?
2. What story is the chart telling?
3. Is the stock hitting resistance?

1. Understanding the trend

The trend is the first thing your chart should tell you. Is the stock trending upwards, downwards, or sideways? The reason you want to know this is that you want to buy stocks that are trending upwards since you are interested in stocks that are increasing value and not decreasing.

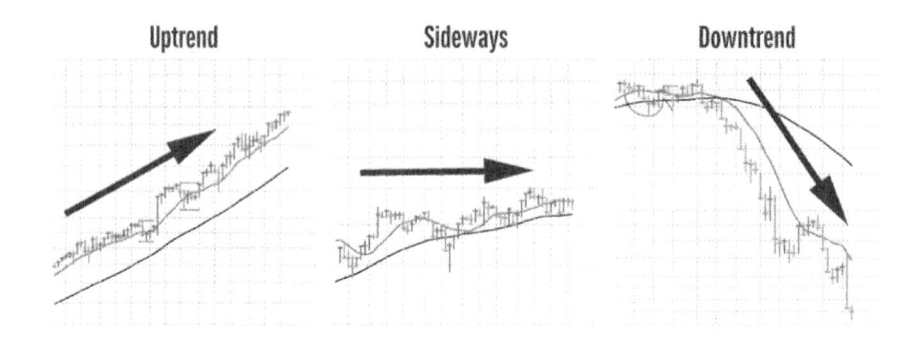

2. Understanding the story behind the chart

When you are looking at a chart, it tells a story beyond whether the stock is trending upwards or downward. A chart will also show you the changes in trading volume and share price of the particular stock. Any drastic changes in volume and price are indicators that you need to be on the lookout for. For instance, if a share on average trades 2 million shares per day, then suddenly spikes to 3 million shares a day and gains 4% in price this change is worth paying attention to.

Increases in price in times of unusually large trading volume indicate that there is institutional demand from large investors. This kind of movement is an indicator that the stock is likely to appreciate in value meaning it is the right time to buy that particular stock.

On the flip side, you may notice that a stock price is dropping in unusually high trading volume. This drop indicates that large investors are dumping shares and naturally you can expect this stock to depreciate in value. This should be your cue not to by that stock because it is likely to keep trending downwards.

In some cases, the price may rise or drop but in unusually light trading volumes. When this happens, it is usually an indicator that large investors are not selling or buying that share aggressively. This means that you may want to hold on to your stock and wait for the trend to change until there is potential for bigger gains.

Understanding the story behind the price changes and trading volumes will also be an important guide on what to expect in terms of trends. This kind of information will guide you on the best time to buy, sell, or hold on to your shares.

3. Look for support or resistance

Looking at the performance of a stock at key points like 10-week and 50- day moving averages can give you an indication of how strong a stock position is. A stock that is finding support will be picked up by large investors when it starts to pull back to the 10-week line. On the flip side, a stock that is finding resistance will drop below the moving average in heavy volume which is an indicator that big investors are dumping the stock.

A stock that is finding support is much stronger and therefore a better pick than one that is finding resistance. Your chart will show you how a stock is performing at its benchmarks and this will give you a clear indication of how strong or weak it is.

Top 3 Most Profitable Chart Patterns

The whole point of reading charts is to help you pick the best stocks, the right time to buy and of course when to sell. As a novice, it is important to understand which chart patterns are the most profitable because these patterns will be an indicator that a particular stock is a safe buy.

The three most profitable chart patterns are the:

I. Cup with handle
II. Double Bottom

III. Flat base

I. Cup with handle

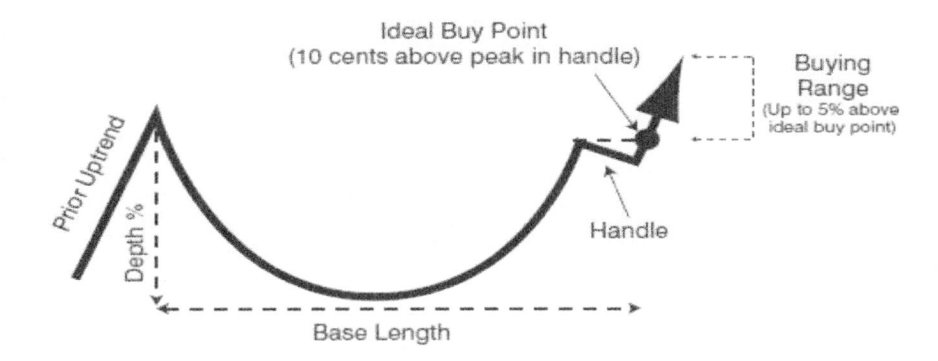

[Diagram: Cup with handle chart pattern showing Prior Uptrend, Depth %, Base Length, Handle, Ideal Buy Point (10 cents above peak in handle), and Buying Range (Up to 5% above ideal buy point)]

This chart pattern will have the following features

- A prior upward trend (30%)
- A base depth of 15-30%
- Seven weeks base length from the first week down
- Five days long handle from the first day down
- A peak in the handle
- Buy range of 5% above the ideal buy point

II. Double Bottom

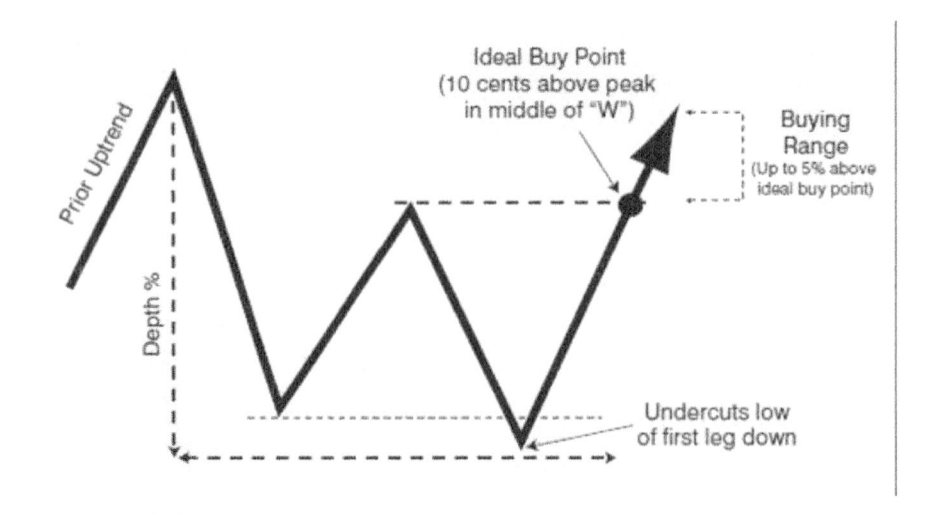

The double bottom chart pattern is typical in volatile markets and it can be the indicator that there will be major price gains in the near future.

A double bottom chart pattern will have the following key features:

- Prior uptrend of at least 30%
- A 40% base depth
- A 7-week base length from the first week down
- A peak in the middle of the two bases (hence the W shape)

III. Flat base

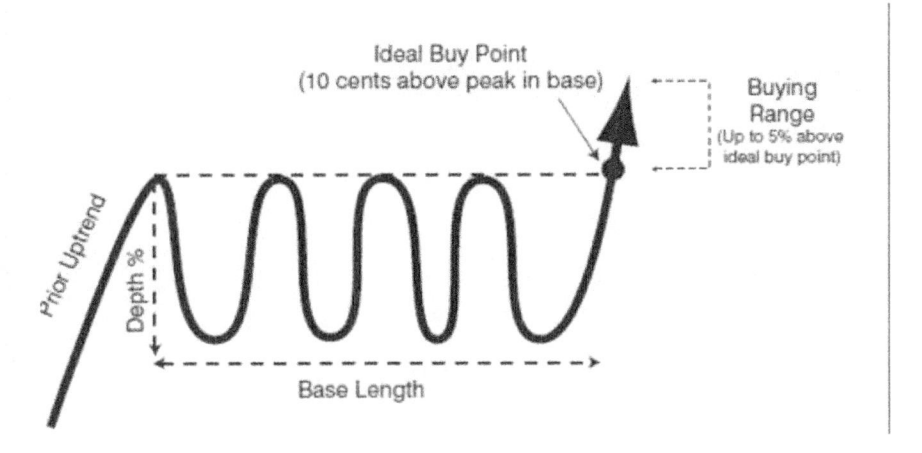

The flat base chart pattern will have the following features:

- A prior uptrend of at least 30%
- Base length of at least five weeks from the first week down
- A base depth of 15 % or less

Ultimately, chart patterns are a reflection of the market. When the market is volatile you should see more double bottom charts. Knowing which chart patterns are likely to set the stage for price gains is a crucial indicator when picking stocks.

Stock Simulators

As a beginner, you want to know that you actually know what you are doing before you start making real trades where your money is on the line. This is why a stock simulator is an important tool for any investor looking to get into the stock market.

A stock simulator allows you to put your trading skills and strategies to the test by allowing you to practice trading without using your money. Most online platforms will offer a stock simulator tools for investors to practice before they start actually investing their money. If you are a novice, it is important to start by trading on a simulator until you find that your strategies are working and helping you pick winning stocks.

What to Look for in a Stock Research Tool

Ultimately the point of a research tool is to enable you to pick the right stocks and make profitable trading moves. For this to happen, the trading tool you have must have the following key features.

- Real-time data

The stock market is constantly changing and these changes often happen from minute to minute. If the information you are getting from your research tool is outdated then that tool is not doing you much good. The ideal research tool should offer real-time stock charting and market streaming. Your simulator tool should also enable you to trade in real-time.

- Customizable

Every trader has their own objectives and trading strategies. An effective trading tool is one that you can customize to reflect your strategy and objectives. This means that it should be flexible and come with options that allow you to create a customized experience.

- Ease of use

All the features in the world are of no use if you do not know how to use them. A user-friendly interphase is therefore an important feature in an effective research tool. You want to spend your time on actual research and not trying to navigate complicated software. Keep it simple by going for research tools that make your job easier.

The Best Stock Research Tools

1. Finviz Stock Screener

- Ideal for beginners and experienced traders
- Easy to use
- Has an impressive range of candlestick charts and visuals
- Comes with 60 plus technical, descriptive, and fundamental characteristics

2. TradeHero App

- Ideal for novices and intermediate trades
- Provides a dummy account for simulated trading
- Using the virtual mode of this app provides a risk-free way to try out your trading strategies

3. TradingView

- Ideal for beginners
- Combines charting and stock screening
- Easy to read charting software

- Provides 100 plus indicators

4. Benzinga Pro

- Easy to use and works for traders of all levels including beginners
- Includes a screener, newsfeed, stock details, signal alerts, top gainers and losers, and many more indicators
- Customizable to fit your needs and strategy

5. The Motley Fool Stock Advisor

- Great for beginners
- Provides you with 2 new monthly expert stock picks if you do not have time to do your own research
- Provides a list of 10 starter stocks for your new portfolio.
- Allows 24/7 monitoring

6. StockFetcher.com

- Ideal for intermediate and expert traders

- Provides candlestick patterns for any stock based on your search criteria
- Offers an impressive range of possibilities and combinations

Chapter 4: Strategies for Long Term Success

In uncertain times like during a pandemic most investors find themselves tempted to pull out of the stock market in an attempt to stave off further losses. However, over time, staying the course has been found to be the wiser course of action during periods of market volatility. In the stock market history, changes in trading patterns have been found to only last as long as the crisis meaning that investors who stay put end up making substantial gains in the long term.

Taking a long-term view of your investment will help you to avoid costly knee jerk reactions in periods of market volatility. Drawing lessons from market downturns experienced in the past such as during the financial crisis in 2008 or the 1990s can help you in understanding how best to position yourself for recovery in times of volatility and downward trends.

Even in volatile conditions, it is still possible to find winning stocks that make good investment sense. Case in point; stocks of companies such as Netflix have appreciated in value since the start of the Coronavirus pandemic. Some pharmaceutical companies and tech giants have also managed to withstand the economic downturn occasioned by the global pandemic. The moral of the story is that for long term investors the stock market is always a good investment avenue. However, it is crucial to be able to pick the right stocks, especially during volatile market conditions.

When to Buy

Picking the right stock significantly increases your profit potential and minimizing your risk. So, it is no surprise that one of the best things you need to understand as a beginner is when to buy. While there is no such thing as a perfect market, there are three key indicators that should tell you that it is the right time to buy into a position.

1. Market direction

There is a common myth in the stock market and unfortunately, many beginners fall into this pitfall. *Fallen Angels Will Go Back Up, Eventually* may be a good title for a movie but as a trading strategy, you want to stay as far away from it as possible. It is not uncommon to find traders picking up shares that are trending downwards with the hope that they will eventually bounce back.

Let's say for example you are considering two stocks. Stock A has fallen from an all-time high of $100 to an all-time low of $50 in the past twelve months. Stock B on the other hand, has seen modest gains over the same time period and gone from $10 to $20. Research has found that most investors will choose stock A despite the fall because they expect it will eventually bounce back. This kind of move is detrimental to your portfolio and could lead to massive losses. Going for stocks that are trending upwards is always a better option because you will buy in at a reasonable price and your investment will increase in value over time.

In short when it comes to buying stocks, always pick the winning horse. While fallen stocks may indeed bounce back eventually, as an investor your goal should be growth and not price. A growing stock bought at a modest cost will eventually translate into better returns on your investment than a down-trending stock bought at a higher cost.

2. Look at the market fundamentals

Company fundamentals are usually a pretty good indicator of how strong a stock is. This means that before you purchase a stock you need to consider the following fundamentals

- Current quarterly and annual earnings – stocks with earnings increases over time are usually a good buy. Gains in earnings are a pretty good indicator that the stock is likely to increase in value and therefore a good pick for you to buy. Go for stocks that average at least a 25% growth in earnings.
- Supply and demand – it is always important to understand how the supply of a particular share compares to its demand. A stock with high trading volumes will indicate strong interest from large investors which is usually a cue that it is the right time to buy. In the same vein, a stock with low trading volumes usually indicates a lack of interest from major players which could signal an upcoming downturn.

- Look for companies that have something new – go for stocks of companies that have something game-changing or new to offer. Historically, stocks of such companies end up being winners because they are at the start of their growth period as opposed to companies that have already peaked and stagnated.

3. Look at the chart action

Technical analysis is an investor's most important tool. Charts will help you understand the best buy points into a stock and whether the particular stock is worth buying into at all. Understanding your charts and knowing which patterns are indicative of winning stocks is crucial in determining the best time to buy a stock.

In a nutshell, there are three cues to check for in a chart that are indicators of high potential stocks.

- The chart pattern or base is preceded by an uptrend.
- The bottom of the base is an area of support, not resistance

- The buy point is based on a former area of resistance.
- The stock punches through the point of resistance in unusually heavy trading volume.

When to Sell

Your exit point is every bit as important as your buy-in point. For most investors figuring out the right time to exit is challenging. On the one hand, you do not want to exit at a loss and on the other, you do not want to sell stocks that are gaining value. So how do you strike a balance that helps to keep your investment portfolio healthy?

1. Go for gains that range from 20 -25%

It is natural to want to wait for a home run and make a huge profit on your investment but in most cases, growth stocks tend to decline or revert to their original position after a 20% increase. This means that waiting for the stock to rise beyond a 25% rise may actually lead you into a decline and you will have missed the opportune selling window.

A great exit strategy from a position is to lock in your gains at 20% and in so doing avoid having the gains disappear when the stock corrects. You can compound those gains by buying into other stocks that are at the beginning of a price run. In this way, you will grow your portfolio substantially over time.

2. Limit your losses using the 8% sell rule

As an investor one of the most important things you can do for your portfolio is learning to limit your losses. That is where it is recommended that you sell a stock if it declines to 8% below what you purchased it for. Using the 8% sell rule helps you put a cap on your loss.

When a stock starts to plummet, there is no telling at what point the decline will stop. This is when it is important to preserve your capital and avoid further losses by selling when the stock starts to fall below 8% of the buying price. Preserving your capital means that even though you have taken a loss you will not lose your entire investment. Think of the 8% sell as a sort of insurance against a devastating blow to your portfolio.

3. Take profits when a stock crashes through a rising trend line

A trend line typically connects three or more price lows over a period of no less than 18 weeks. When a stock breaks away from the trend line that is usually a cue to sell. A break from the trendline will come with other sell signals such as a sustained drop. It is important to always make sure that your trend line covers the appropriate amount of time, at least 18 weeks, to avoid selling too early.

Staying Ahead of the Curve

Many people have built wealth and kept it by investing in the stock market but in the same vain many people have lost money in the stock market. What separates winning traders from losing traders is simply the kinds of strategies and the mindset they take to the stock market. Ultimately, the stock market favors those who are looking to build wealth over time over those trying to make a quick buck.

If you want to make money and more importantly keep it when trading the stock market, there are numerous strategies that you can use. However, like everything else, you do not need to use every strategy out there. A wise trader picks the strategy that best suits their trading objectives and trading plan. If you are saving for retirement, it is unlikely that your strategy will be exactly the same as someone saving for a major outlay five years down the line. This is why it is important that trading strategies are not viewed as a one size fits all affair.

As your experience in the stock market grows you will undoubtedly pick up numerous strategies. However, for beginners keeping it simple is the way to go and there are 3 key strategies that you need to keep in mind.

1. Dollar-cost averaging

For both new investors and seasoned traders, dollar-cost averaging is an effective strategy. This strategy works as a risk management tool and also as a tool to help you build trading consistency and discipline. The concept of dollar-cost averaging involves investing regular automated investments made over time as opposed to lump-sum investments.

When you use dollar-cost averaging as a strategy, you will avoid the risks that come with poor market timing. Regular spread out investments means that you will capture stock prices at both high levels and low levels. This will offset ant possible consequences of poor timing.

To use the dollar-cost averaging strategy, you will need to figure out the following:

- The amount of capital you want to invest
- The frequency of investment e.g. monthly, quarterly, semi-annually, etc.

For instance, you can invest $500 monthly instead of investing $60000 as a lump sum. What this does is safeguard from the effects of market volatility by enabling you to buy into the market gradually and over an extended period of time. Ultimately this reduces your risk exposure. Dollar-cost averaging is also a good strategy for beginners because it helps you invest consistently. This means you will not be tempted to make impulsive trades because your investments are on an automated schedule.

2. Growth Investing

Growth investing means going for stocks that have strong indicators that they will be the next big thing. When you use growth investing as a strategy it means that you are evaluating a stock not just based on its current price in the market but also based on its potential for growth. This is where you pay attention to companies that are offering revolutionary or out of the box products or services. Think of disrupters such as Uber or Airbnb that took the market by storm and revolutionized the industries in which they operate.

For instance, the increase in investor interest in stocks of companies such as Tesla has grown steadily over the past few years. This has been informed by the realization that consumer interest in electric cars is growing and set to keep increasing. Investors who were able to identify this emerging interest in electric cars at the beginning of the trend have undoubtedly made huge gains and seen the portfolios grow significantly.

The pay off in growth investing is that you catch the stock at the beginning of its upward trend. This means that your investment has a chance to realize substantial gains as the stock is set to keep growing. However, for beginners, it is important to make the distinction between growth investing and speculating. Speculating is when you invest expecting drastic price fluctuations to result in gains. However, with speculation, the risk is always equal to the potential payoff which makes speculative trading more or less like gambling.

To identify a growth stock look for steady gains in earnings and revenue. These are usually strong indicators that the particular stock is set to keep increasing in value over time. Keeping abreast of what is going on in different industries will also help you spot the next big thing early enough to get in at the start of the upward trend.

3. Prioritize managed funds over individual stocks
Perhaps one of the most effective strategies a beginner can employ in the stock market is ensuring that the majority of their investment is on index funds and EFTs as opposed to individual stocks. When you invest in

pooled funds you may not own shares directly in the company but you end up with a diversified portfolio that has limited risk exposure.

Index funds and EFTs are managed by experts and they relieve you of the hassle of going through hours of analysis and research to come up with the best stock to purchase. Ideally, your portfolio should be primarily made up of mutual funds, EFTs, and index funds. A minimal percentage of your investment should be on individual stocks because they carry a higher risk.

The main advantage of pooled funds such as EFTs is that they combine diverse stocks in such a way that the winners end up balancing out the losers. This means that your investment portfolio will keep growing steadily even in volatile market conditions. The other plus that comes with going with managed funds is that this is a passive form of investment that does not require you to keep buying and selling stocks. Your portfolio is managed by experts so you have the luxury of watching your portfolio grow as you get on with your life.

Limiting your individual stock investments to no more than 10% of your investment portfolio means that even if you pick a losing stock, the loss will not make a huge dent in your investment portfolio. It is also important to note that passively managed accounts end up costing you less in fees and transaction costs as opposed to actively managed accounts.

Ultimately your goal as a beginner is to pick a strategy that will see you build wealth over time. There is no better way to do this than by managing your risks by prioritizing managed funds and making them a larger percentage of your investment portfolio.

The 4-Step Routine for Picking Winners

When it comes to trading having a routine helps you to stay disciplined and consistent in your trading. It also simplifies the process for you as a new investor by creating a clear process that helps you research your stocks and come up with the best picks.

1. Gather your research tools

The best starting point when researching a stock is the company's financials. Financials will give you indicators such as growth in earnings over a specified period, revenues, and expenses. These are useful parameters in determining how strong a stock is. If a company has solid financials, chances are its position in the market is strong and it is likely to trend upward.

Weak financial such as drops in earnings over time are indicators that a company may be headed for a downturn in the market. Your research tools will provide you with the information that you need to guide you when picking which shares will make a sound investment and which ones you should pass up.

2. Narrow your focus

To make your process more effective, it is important to narrow down your prospects to a manageable number. Do not try to follow 10 or more stocks at a time because this will probably mean that you will miss crucial details. If you are using charts or stock screeners in the first step, use them to narrow down your focus to a few stocks that meet your criteria.

Once you have picked three or four stocks to work with, you can then narrow down your analysis to four key areas.

- Company revenue
- Net income
- Earnings per share
- Price-earnings ratio
- Return on equity

These parameters will give you a clearer picture of the financial status of the company. By making comparisons of these parameters among the stocks you are considering investing in, it will be much easier to spot the stronger picks based on their financials.

3. Get into the qualitative research

After getting an overview of the financials, qualitative research will give you an overview of the company beyond the financials. This is especially important if you are looking to do growth investing by picking stocks with high growth potential. Your qualitative research should focus on the following key areas.

I. What industry is the company in; how does the company make money, is it an emerging market, is it an industry disrupter, does the business make sense to you?

II. Does the company stand out amongst its competitors; does it have a competitive advantage that makes its growth potential high?

III. What is the leadership of the company like; does it have a solid reputation, is it well managed, Is the leadership embroiled in wrangles or scandal?

IV. What are the potential risks; are the company's products and services likely to be overtaken by technology, is the market getting saturated with similar products?

These details will provide you with a wholesome view of the strength of a particular stock based on the qualitative research that you have conducted. Remember that indicators go beyond financial to prospects, growth potential, and even possible risks.

4. Build a well-informed narrative

The final step is to combine your research from steps 1, 2 & 3 to get the complete story behind the stock. For beginners, it is easy to get caught up in the technical analysis and forget that the fundamentals also have an impact on the performance of a stock. By following these 4-step process when researching stocks, you will cover all the necessary bases.

While there is no fool-proof way of predicting how a stock will perform in the long run, any successful trader will tell you that proper analysis and research is the most effective way to pick winners. Going on a hunch or following the momentum in the market may get you gains once in a while. However, to achieve long term gains and build a well-performing portfolio, you have to priorities effective research and analysis over speculation.

The stock market does not discriminate. Whether you start with millions or hundred, there is room for every kind of investor in the stock market. What makes the difference between the traders who succeed in the long term and those who do not, has less to do with the capital and more to do with the process and strategies used. Many have built long term wealth in the stock market and even more, keep their money in stocks. This is not a coincidence. When it comes to creating and sustaining wealth, you will be hard-pressed to find an investment that beats the stock market.

Conclusion

Online trading platforms have done a tremendous job of making the stock market accessible to all types of investors. You do not need to be wall street big wig or a business mogul to make money in the stock markets. Increasingly, people are turning modest investments into sizable nest eggs that guarantee them financial freedom in the future.

If you have been daunted by the thought of analyzing and researching stocks, you now have the knowledge that you need to get started. This coupled with the wealth of resources available on trading platforms and apps will give you the head start you need to start your journey to financial freedom. The sense of security that comes from knowing that you have a financial plan for your future will almost always outweigh any sacrifices you need to make today in order to start investing.

Moguls like Warren Buffet have made most of their wealth in the stock markets and this if anything is proof that there is money to be made in trading stocks. Whatever your financial goals are, there are few investments that offer the security and long-term return on investments that stock market investing does. The ease of getting started in stock trading makes stock market investing an easy choice if you are looking for an accessible and affordable venture to invest your money in.

The information in this book is designed to help anyone who wants to get started in the stock market but has no idea where to start. We hope that you have gathered enough knowledge to make the first step. The value of time in stock market investing cannot be overstated. While it is never too late to start investing, the best time to start is now.

Long term investments such as stocks rely on the power of time to make significant returns on your investment so the longer you wait to start, the more you lose in terms of compound interest. Since you have already taken the first step by reading this book, the next step should be easy. Find an online trading platform to open a trading account with and start putting the knowledge and strategies you have learned to good use.

Ultimately, the one regret that most people have in their later years is that they did not start saving for the future early enough. You have a chance to write a different financial future for yourself by starting your investment journey today. Whether you are an active investor who wants to get down in the trenches and make your own trades or a passive investor looking for a hassle-free experience, we have given you all the information you need to pursue either of these paths.

A better financial future awaits you if you will but take the first step!

Printed in Great Britain
by Amazon